Dinosaur-Hearted

by Ra Avis

A Silver Star Laboratory Publication

ISBN-13: 978-1-945681-00-4

Printed in the United States of America

Published by Silver Star Laboratory : AuthorPowered.com

Cover Design by Joshua Stroder.

"There Be Dinos" concept illustration by Frank Stangel.

Dinosaur-Heart Illustration and Sign Board Art by Ra Avis.

Griefjoy Matchstick, pg IV, by Jewelle Weston.

Edited by Jessie Stevens and William S. Friday.

Background Photography provided by Unsplash photographers: Tim Arterbury, Samuel Zeller, Khara Woods, Hal Gatewood, Charles Deluvio, Scott Webb, Andrew Ridley, Namroud Gorguis, Juha Lakaniemi, Reiner Knudsen, Britt Felton, Jarrod Reed, Alexej Simonenko, Anton Darius, Annie Spratt, Mauro Bighin, Bruno Ramos Lara, Caroline Grondin, Sharon Benton, Dan Cook, Ben Hershey, Danny Howe, Jacky Watt, Patrick Tomasso, Chris Barbalis, Frank McKenna, Kimberly Farmer, Sonja Punz.

Dedicated to Mamasaur

who still recognizes my heart

even after the world filled it up with beauty,

broke it into pieces,

and glued it back together with glittered scales.

For those we've lost:

"I didn't have the words, so I filled this page with stars." - K. Curtis

acknowledgments

Many of these writings were originally shared outside of Rarasaur blog. Thank you to Sreejit Poole, Makala Kozo Hattori, Jonathon Hilton, Matthew Blashill, Jewelle Weston, Goldy, Brother Jon Hager, and Jaded for lending me their space so I could rest my words.

Best Beloveds — you make everything possible. I am graced by your humor and love. I am honored and humbled by your readership and support.

Jessie, Jeanette, Erica — you are some of the most dinosaur-hearted women I have ever met. I am so very thankful for your daily friendship. I love you.

Diamond Mike — thank you for showing me how to stay inspired by the world.

Anthony, Bill, Deb, Josh, and Matt — thank you for being on my team.

Owen — with none of the hyperbole so expected in my writing, I want to share a few truths with you and those who read this: *This book would not exist if you did not exist.   I would no longer exist if you did not exist.* Thank you for not letting me float away.

Dave — thud.

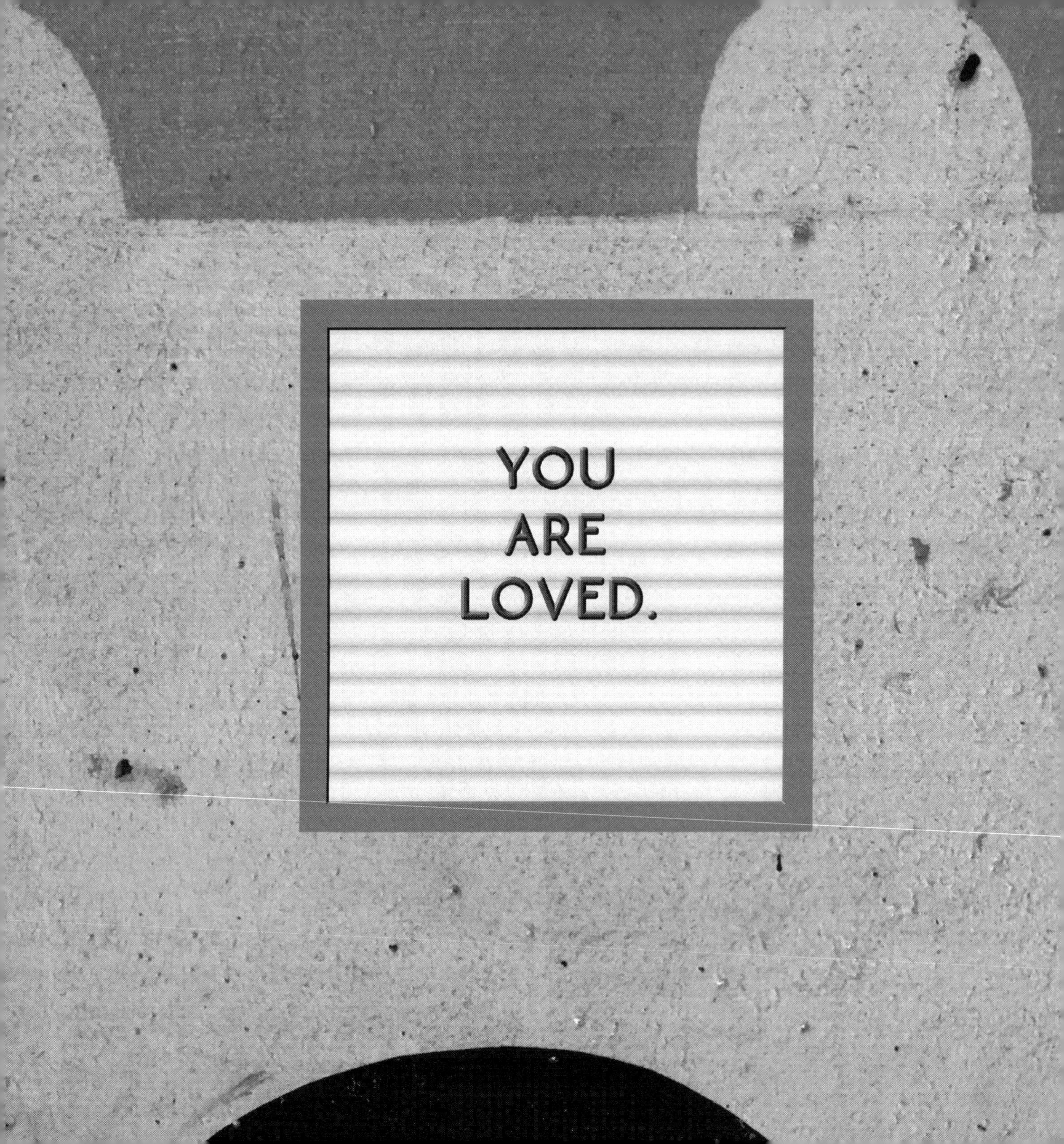
YOU
ARE
LOVED.

contents

Dinosaur-Hearted 1

Active Love 5

Life and Death 11

Gently Now 15

All the Little Lights 17

In Truth 21

What Happened 23

Thud 25

No Detours 27

Blessings 29

Companion Souls 31

Good Morning 37

Faith Does 41

Keep It Up 45

EGBO 47

Hand Made 49

You Are Loved 53

Tangled Universe 55

What If 59

One Second 61

Best Things 63

All Beans 65

Freedom Whistles 67

Goals 71

Endings Fold 73

Woven World 75

Happiness Stays 77

World Pained 79

Let's Go 81

Just Broken 83

Because I've Had Enough 87

Wild Heart 89

Dreams Sparkle 93

Good Luck 95

Look Up 97

The Knowing 99

Bleeding Gratitude 101

Untold Stories 103

Teardrop Confetti 109

Family Time 111

Home Rooted 113

Poetry Passing 115

Mulberry Street 119

New Year 123

Early Girl 125

Frightfully Wondrous 127

A Note from Rara 131

YOU ARE
FRIGHTFULLY
WONDROUS.

dinosaur-hearted

Maybe nobody can see past your heart.
It's so big.

Maybe nobody can see past the spikes in it,
the ones so asymmetrical that some days
you're thrown off-balance, that some days,
your heart beats with a limp, that some
days, you're dangerous to touch.

Maybe nobody is sure how to handle
your claws, your roar, your teeth that
you snap like a drowning poet,
your blue that you wear like skin.

Maybe you feel like they're staring behind you, at the footsteps you left when you carried heavy things like big love and tall sadness.

Maybe they've noticed you leave no footsteps at all now, like a vanished one.
an extinct creature,
a dinosaur.

Maybe you are a dinosaur,
basically.

Maybe you have a dinosaur heart, and it's supposed to be big. and it's supposed to be spiked, and it's supposed to scare people a little.

the ones who should be scared, but not you. Never you.

Don't be afraid to be dinosaur - hearted. You are not alone, my love. We are not extinct.

We have seen things so heartbreaking our blood held its breath, our pulse learned to shatter. So heartbreaking, we learned how to store kindness in our veins, how to love through a cage, how to trust the compass in our bandaged hearts.

We have always found the way.
We have always known the way.
We have always been the way.

You don't need a map or a guide or a dream, you simply need your heart. It is yours today, and today will always be yours.

active love

I don't remember learning how to love, originally. I only remember the origins of little love-habits.

I remember holding onto my stuffed elephant, tucked safely in my right arm always — a light grey beast with pink-tinted ears. He must've been a foot tall, if he could have stood on his own, but he couldn't.

He needed me.

His fur was worn down, paper thin, from all the hugs.

"If you sneeze too hard, you'll knock his stuffing out," my big brother would say, so I learned to sneeze into the crook of my left arm.

Obviously I learned to love before that memory, or, why else would the cloth have been so loved that my poor little elephant literally wore its insides on its out? Why else would I remember my brother the way I do? Magical, certainly. Immortal, maybe.

I dropped that elephant in the mud one day, when my big brother finally, finally, finally came home from college, because I had to run as fast as I could toward him and I would not allow a single thing to slow me down.

I knew the difference then, between some types of love.

I had a habit of love then, already — no less permanent than my habit of sneezing.

Eventually I'd stop holding a stuffed animal in my right arm. Eventually I'd find a hundred other types of love — some I ran toward, some I left behind.

I'm still learning, but that's how most of the big things in life work. The learning never stops, and sometimes it's hard to remember how it all got started.

I don't remember learning how to write.

I remember lettering, of course. The almost-religious importance of a straight T and a dotted lower case i. I was painstakingly slow, as I am with most things that depend on the invisible thread between my mind and my hand. I re-member the large paper and the lines that run across the sheet — a solid blue, a dashed blue, a solid pink.

Who decides these things?

Not me.

I don't make the rules of school paper design, or life, or love, or writing. I just learn them.

In the 7th grade, I memorized prepositional phrases, employed onomatopoeia, practiced hyperbole.

Around the bridge, over the bridge, under the bridge... The bird squeaks, the bridge creaks, the wind rustles them both the same. The little girl scratches her pencil, across the paper, until she can ink her way into bigger classrooms, until she can type her way into deeper laugh wrinkles.

I remember typing my first story into a word processor, and letting it grade my work. It was riddled with flaws — too many emdashes, too short of paragraphs. Fragments. Passive voice.

All the feathers
on the bird
sparkled.
And — oh! —
what joy it brought the sun,
to see another
shine
so bright.

That poem is passive if I intend for the focus to be on the bird, but of course I don't. That is a story about the sun, about a feather, about a friendship. That is a story about love.

I don't remember learning how to love, but there are tiny love-habits that have stitched into my skin like feathers. They fly away from me sometimes — but then, joyfully, every so often, I grow a new one.

I don't remember learning how to write, but I notice my habits, the way the sun sees the light of the bird, the way a good listener can see how the wind speaks to everyone just the same. A sentence fragment here. Passive voice there. This sparkles, that doesn't.

I don't remember learning how to write or love, originally, but I know that I am still learning. I am still loving, and I am still holding my loves oh-so-tightly in my strongest arm.

That's where you are — my readers, my teachers, my friends.

And you are loved.

You are loved.

You are loved.

That sentence is in the passive voice, if you want to believe it is about me. But of course it's not.

It's about all the many beginnings we live even after we forget our first beginnings. It's about what we want to remember when we can't really remember anything at all. It is about the stuffing that stays inside of us, no matter how hard anyone sneezes, and the feathers that sparkle on us, even when the sun closes her eyes. It's about the love that drops us in the mud, and the love that pulls us out.

It's about why we keep learning, why we keep writing, and why we bother to keep loving at all.

So, for me, for always—

it is about you.

I hope you remember it.

life and death

I grew up on a farm, the sort where nothing obstructs the view of the sunrises or sunsets. The sort where there's more acres than people, more cows than buildings.

One day, after a bit of a windstorm, I filled a bucket with well-water and splashed it upward and over my roof. There were leaves gathering there, and I decided it was better that they wash down the drain now, rather than wait for the next part of their journey. If they stayed there, they'd turn into a dangerous home for a bird that didn't know better, or they'd turn into mulch for a roof that would eventually give way and join them in rot.

The water rushed through the drain, gurgling as it struggled to move past all the debris I knocked from the rooftop, finally pushing it all out in front of my feet. There was a pebble, and a slimy tangle of unnameable gunk, and a few leaves, and, on top of it all, was a giant monarch butterfly. A dead one.

I must have killed her — drowned her with the force of my splash, with the purpose of my urgency.

I died then, too, for just for a second.

It was as if a motionless butterfly hugged its wings over me — a sticky wet tarp over my heart — suffocating it for a beat, at least.

I couldn't stop staring at her wings. Undamaged by the storm, simply motionless and beautiful — the perfection of them making my stomach roll. There
were ugly things in that pile, too. Tangles riddled with gunk — ugly ugly things.
The sort that make strong adults choke on air, the sort that make it so no one
ever wants to look too deeply into the dark abyss of their drains. But it was
the fallen beauty that stopped time, it always is. An object in motion stays in
motion, and an object paused is contagious too.

Death is coded into us.

A spider knows how to spin at birth, and we know how to die. It is our web,
that we spin inside ourselves. We spend a lifetime with that trick up our
sleeves, just to make sure it surprises everyone else when we play it out.

Abracadabra!

Once a moment of time dies, it stays dead. Time waits for no one, least of
all itself. It becomes a leftover — a fragment — and our hearts aren't built to
process that while living, so a part of us dies with that moment.

In that way, carrying death with us is a critical part of living. It is a web spun from the gossamer threads of our ancestry. That web pulls and snaps inside of us when we recognize loss. It bounces inside with stretch and agony — pushed and tugged by the unstoppable buoyancy of living.

And we are tiny robots, trying to process it all into the binary. Sometimes it breaks us a little bit, sometimes we crash. Nothing lasts forever, and some things are built for their eventual end.

We recognize even the echoes of death, in our core.

We recognize ourselves in the patterns of the universe so that we can continue the code.

We are temporary machines, born with the understanding that we will survive all our storms except the final one.

It is why we die with the ones we love, and the fallen ones we see. It's why we live in the ones we love, and ache for the loss of lives we never knew.

We reason life and death into now and then, before and after, ones and zeroes — and some part of us can't help but hope for the possibility that might exist between those two points.

It's why it is so very important to let yourself break a little bit, over *every* little bit. It puts a hiccup in the code, a space between the binary. It gives a little more elasticity to the web inside of us — the one spun from magic and grief, instinct and love.

We are temporary machines, but the program we run is eternal. We are each other's ancestors.

And all those butterflies that are washed away? All those dead seconds that time left behind?

They aren't wasted.

They aren't forgotten.

We carry them forward.

The final fog of a magic trick, passed from one generation to the next.

They will be the spun-strength of somebody's life. The birth-wealth of some-body's human inheritance.

They will be somebody's magic.

gently now

Close the door gently when you do.
It is, after all, how you made it through.

Be soft with whatever happened to you.
Close the door gently, when you do.

Keep your heart open — bold and true.
It is, after all, how you made it through.

HEART
MUSCLES
HAVE
MEMORY.

all the little lights

I sparked my first match when I was six years old, in the harvest season, for the Festival of Lights. It was a matchbook stick and my big brother helped me tear it off. The cardboard end was unnaturally angled, and bent even further when I gently slid it against the rough striker on the back of the folded book.

My fingers already smelled and I wrinkled my nose. *Sulfer dioxide*, my big brother said, answering the unasked question, and I repeated the words with a grownup nod.

The light didn't appear, so he patiently instructed me to try it again. I did, quickly this time, with ferocity and purpose. I still remember the flame sputtering to life — as if it had always been there, just waiting for me to bring the shape of it to reality.

I never really even notice matches anymore. But back then, it was new — the air was heavy with the smell of burning, my fingers were warm, and my heart was racing. I lit the little wax candle in front of me, and then quickly blew the burn of the matchstick away. The smoke was a dark foggy place where a light once blazed, and I breathed it in as I watched my candle dance in the moonlight.

It was just a little light, but even a little light pushes back the darkness.

I knew there were thousands of little girls and boys doing the same thing that night, throughout the world. All our lights were little — like our hands, like our lives — but we all knew there was nothing like a million little lights to brighten a path.

We all share the same darkness, even though we each come face to face with different shapes of it. We all share the same light.

Loss is a darkness many of us have touched, shaped like what no longer is.

I know the shape of the missing spaces that make up my dark expanse. And I know you have a dark spot, too.

This day might be the day that it first appeared. This year, last year, or maybe even a dozen years ago, or three dozen — it doesn't matter. Time doesn't fight darkness, only light does.

I don't know the shape of your dark spaces, and I'm not sure I'll ever have a right to know. I don't have the right words to give you, and I'm not absolutely sure they exist at all.

I know there's nothing I can do to fill the blanks in your heart with substance, and I don't know you would want me to even if I could.

But I do know what I knew back then, in the fall of my sixth year of life — that we share the same darkness, and we share the same light, and the flame is only waiting on us to call itself into reality.

So for you, today, I am striking a match, in hopes it softens the edges of your dark. In hopes it illuminates the you that I know and love and see — even now when your heart is so entrenched in the empty. In hopes that thousands of other lights are lit for you too, and that all those little lights together push the darkness back just far enough for you to take one tiny step forward past tonight, straight toward a promise we all share:

the dawn of a better tomorrow.

in truth

Imagine a fat glass of milk, floating in space.

Now imagine the glass part is not there. You are looking at a cylinder made entirely of milk, sitting in the middle of the cosmos.

No matter where you are on Earth, you can look up and see this well of milk. If you climb a tall enough mountain, or fly a small enough plane, you can approach the milk — you can touch it, smell it, or even take some.

No matter how much people take, the well of milk remains.

That milk is truth.

Some people go on with their lives, never looking up, never wondering what it is, or what it means to them.

Others dedicate their lives to understanding its essence.

Some people reach into the well with their bare hands, dripping milk from their palms, desperate to understand it in the fleeting moments before it slips between their fingers.

Others rely on ceremony and declare the truth to be divine.

They use a jewel-encrusted goblet, or a clay mug, or a disposable cup to sample it — never seeing how the vehicle they have chosen imposes limitations on truth itself.

Still others deny its divinity and measure it with the slow tools available to their ever-growing understanding of science.

The same milk that watches over an oblivious child on her way to school is the same milk found in a golden chalice. The same milk found in a test tube is the same milk found on the floor, splattered from the dirty grasp of a hobo.

Truth is neither a chameleon nor a con artist, and it does not share its secrets lightly.

It is ageless, eternal, and unchanging — but it is not all there is.

There is Perception, a fugitive who makes a mockery of the laws of truth. It whispers to anyone who seeks the well, singing a song of righteousness, power, and superiority. The song dances and delights, but if you listen carefully, past the cacophony...

Truth is bellowing, echoing the earth, playing a drumbeat that sets the rhythm for everything that is and was.

what happened

What happened there?   ... life happened.

I ran so fast I left bits of skin and blood behind on a four lane freeway in Seattle. I bled into a bus in Jersey, but the bus driver had a Green Lantern bandage in his metal lunch box so it didn't scar as much as it could have.

I was slapped by a dog. Thick claws against soft human skin. Drank out of a straw for three months and called it a win. We lived too far from the hospital to get stitches unless it was a dire necessity, but dried tobacco held my face in place even if it did cost me my dimples.

Stitches had been a dire necessity only a year before. Double-digit tallies of thread, sewn in by a doctor who looked like Mr. Magoo and smelled like mint peppermint patties.

A stapler, wielded poorly by an astronaut. A luggage buckle, dropped by a handsome bellman. A concession stand, on the outskirts of a volleyball game.

A plastic spoon at a funeral. A saran wrap machine in a gas station. A giant tub of cobbler in state prison kitchen-- that light burn ripped itself into an open wound as I stood in front of a flaming garbage fire the next day.

Worrying too much. Thinking too hard. Working too long.   It's a wrinkle, not a scar, but good luck sinking the truth of that into my thick skin.

Piercings I changed my mind about. The chicken pox. A pinch from a sliding door as I watched my baby brother's first steps. Cat scratch. Bee sting. Splinter from a treehouse I loved, a treehouse I hated, a dog house that never housed a dog. Splinter from a chicken coop that housed a zillion chickens — and me, for a day.

A bathroom counter, once. Twice. Okay, three times.

That one? Just a birthmark, a mole, a beauty mark. They say it makes me royalty, magical, hallmarked by God.   They say it makes me cursed, fate-kissed, pinpointed by a Universe on a path of destruction.

The time I was outside.   The time I was inside. The time I was loved, and the time I was forgotten. It's just a wrinkle, a mark, a fold, a cut, a line, a dot, a spot. It's just the same story, over and over again.

I ran so fast that I left bits of myself behind, everywhere.

What happened there?   Life happened.

Aren't I lucky?

thud.

The wild waves of your story crash
against mine. In a drop, I see your
depth. In your storm, I taste hope,
purified by the salt of pain.

Beyond your horizon, I hear our
sameness.

It is deafening.
It <u>thuds</u>.

It splashes with all the right words,
said in just the right way. It is a
mantra born from a language we
all speak before we speak any
language at all.

Listen when you are able.
Listen when you are in need.

Let it flow through you and carry
the truth to your whole ocean:

I hear you. I see you.
Thud.

no detours

We took a detour this morning. We went the long way around — past the ocean whose distance from me can be measured in single digit minutes.

Maybe it's because the stars I was born under, or the categories my personality fits in, or one of the million other things that define us in subtle or arguably-non-existent ways, but I don't like detours.

I feel the weight of them on my chest, flattening and numbing my heart. It doesn't matter if the way is pretty, I worry to myself — *it is not the way*.

This morning — tired and anxious — I searched for something that would remind me to be still in the middle of my chaos and found an old reminder to myself.

It is frightening to lose what you have already found. It is disconcerting to seek what you already know — but maybe the turn you took is exactly where you already were meant to go. Maybe the person you are becoming is exactly the person you always were.

Maybe there's no such thing as detours, maybe there's only The Way, and maybe you are headed in exactly the right direction.

blessings

I light this candle for all humankind.
For peace and freedom in earth and mind.
May we carry love forward.
May we leave hate behind.

I light this candle for hopeful clichés.
For childhood wishes that amuse and amaze.
May joy lift us up.
May grace ease our days.

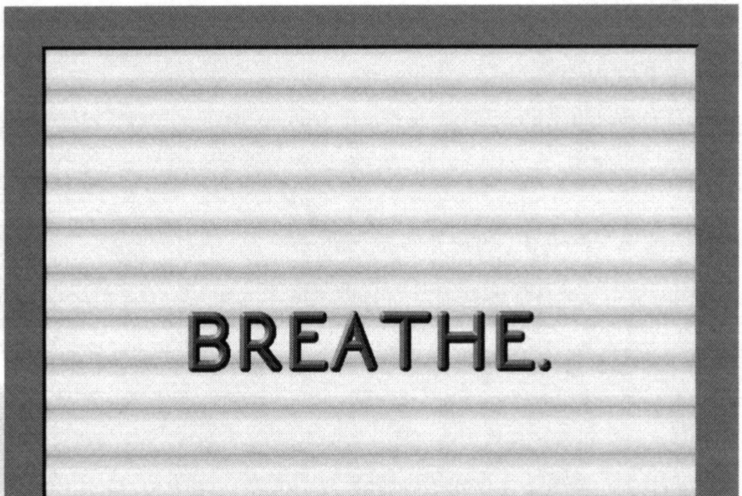
BREATHE.

companion souls

He pulls up again. This was the third or maybe fourth time in as many months. Different time of day, different street, but I think I am wearing the same clothes. I'm not bothered, but only because he won't remember me.

I slide into his car.

"Now, now, now, how do you say that name of yours?" he asks.

"It's Ra." I say.

"I wasn't sure," he said, "if it was pronounced in the masculine."

"I know, right? Ray versus Rah, either seems as likely — but it *is* Ra, even though I am female and it is a man's name. Well, I suppose it was a God's name first." I chuckle at the misunderstanding.

He shakes his head, "Ah, but yes, yes, Raet is a goddess. So it is both genders, and no genders, and it is powerful."

"In fact," I say, "Ra is short for Radhika. She is a deity, too. Just another companion goddess, though."

"It is power, still, always." Mr. Famous says, smiling, though I can't see it. It is the sort of smile that changes the energy of a room. I can feel it.

The conversation is comforting to me, like watching Mr. Rogers slip on his cardigan. We've done this before, we'll do it again. He never remembers me, some people never do, but he never forgets these streets. He follows the star on his map, and never asks if I know where I'm going.

I don't.

My friend is next to me in the backseat. His foot isn't tapping, like normal, he isn't looking over the seat to the road. Mr. Famous puts him at ease for some reason, and I wish, not for the first time, that I could request specific drivers. I'd rather wait 15 minutes for Mr. Famous, than drive with someone else who arrives instantly.

Like me, he is a good companion.

* * *

Raet is a companion goddess, a consort. Radhika is, as well. Some existences are built to foil others, to complement, to meld.

"Don't you want to be the biggest thing in your universe?" so many people ask through inference. The books all say that if you reach high enough, others will let you stand on them. This life is your ship, you can be the captain, you can be the horizon, you can be the North Star, you can be the sails.

My spine is a strong one, so strong that it knows how to bend.

My mind is a strong one, so strong that it knows how to open.

I like to flex like the wind that pushes you forward. I like my molecules to dance fast, to change shape.

I like to be the companion.

I am mutable by nature, but there is power in my nature — still, always — just ask my namesakes.

Just ask Mr. Famous.

* * *

Late night, same day, this time I think he recognizes me. It has only been a few hours. It is raining now, and the droplets fall on the windshield as we move through the streets of Long Beach, in smooth contrast to the sharp jazz playing through the speakers.

He doesn't speak, but I know he is paying attention. When I close my eyes, he turns up the music loud enough that the saxophone might be behind me, and when I open my eyes to count the raindrops, he lowers the sounds of the car so the splashes can have their own chance to serenade.

I can't see his smile, but I know it is there.

This stranger is good company, I think, and he enjoys the art of good companionship, like me. Like my namesakes.

I wonder if his own name holds a similar story, but I don't know his real one. The app says only that he is called Mr. Famous.

I'm tempted to ask:

Now now now, how do you say that name of yours?

But it doesn't matter. Companions do not have eyes for companions, sidekicks don't bond with other sidekicks, we are searching for the ones that do not bend. We are driving toward the ones that you can fold yourself around. The ones you cannot forget, the ones no one can forget.

We are Alfred, the butler, waiting on our Hero. We are human strays, racing toward a time machine, trusting in our Doctor. We are Radhika, resting on a muddy pasture, looking up at our King. We are Raet, the solar goddess, praying for our Sun. We are Mr. Famous, the driver, following our Star.

We are secondaries in a universe that idolizes the origins. We are bylines in a village that wants to stretch everything into a headline. We are raindrops in a world that thinks the ground is stronger because it does not weep.

We are waiting for someone, or something, to be alongside.

The rain has stopped singing, we pull up to my driveway and exchange gratitudes.

I step out into the mud.

The water has shaped the earth just as it likes it, and the earth does not mind at all. The ground is powerful enough to hold the rain, and the rain is powerful enough to be held. Neither are concerned with who appears to be more.

The one in the sky, shedding brightness, is not always the one who makes the light.

The sails on the ship are not always what guides it. The one who is driving is not always the one who picked the star to follow.

But sometimes things are exactly as they seem, and that is perfectly beautiful, too. Power is a shifting thing, a subtle thing, a still thing, an *always* thing.

Just ask Mr. Famous.

good morning

Welcome to the world. We're all so happy to have you here.

Since you've been born, the sun smiles a little more widely. The fog dances a little more wildly. The ocean splashes a little outside her lines. The stars stay out a little past their bedtime.

They're happy they get to see you now.   You are very important.

There's never been a *you* before, so every time you smile or yawn, they are reminded:

Goodness can be born in a blink. Champions can be made in a moment.

Little feet can make big impact.

The world is birthing her own medicine — little hands that will become bigger hands, bigger hands that might just refuel her with joy and health.

Anything is possible.

It's safe to be a little brave.

But of course you know that, you're too new to have forgotten.

Could you hear your mom's thoughts when you lived inside her? She doesn't share them with everyone. You're very lucky.

Do you remember floating? We all forget eventually. You're very blessed.

Maybe one day, if you stay gentle, you'll be privileged to the quiet thoughts of a graced thinker again.

Maybe one day, if you work hard, you can visit the stars that have always loved you so.

Does it feel oh-so-very wonderful to be free, and yet oh-so-very terrifying?

I understand.

Does being alive in such a different world feel exciting and uncertain, all at once?

I understand.

You're too young for the story of why I understand so well. The story of why you didn't hear my laugh while you were floating. The story of why you haven't heard my voice just yet.

You're too small for big stories, which is why you'll have to find a book or twenty to love. Keep listening. Become a strong reader, so you'll be able to carry any story you want, no matter how young you are or how heavy it is.

You will get bigger, little one, but you are small now, so I will tell you a small story:

Everything's gonna be okay. You are loved.

It is a gift, yours for the keeping. You're welcome to plant it deep in the Earth when your little feet become big feet, when your little hands become big hands, so that you can make sure your sun, and your stars, your ocean, and your fog know, too.

I know it for certain, even though I don't know much about life or how to live it, and by the time you're old enough to really understand what I mean by that, I'll probably know even less.

But I do know how very loved you are. I loved you with all my heart before I even knew you were coming.

And I also know, it's okay to be a little brave, because no matter how a day feels or a page in a story sounds....

Everything's gonna be okay.

Okay — or better. Better, and gentle.

Gentle and brave.

Just like you.

Good morning, little one.

Welcome to the world.

faith does

I believe in the power of fairy tales, and it has never mattered to me if someone else understands why.

It doesn't matter if the forest was really as dark as they said, or how old Goldilocks was, or whether or not it was a wolf or a fox. It only matters that the story was heard and a lesson was learned. Stories make sense out of science and carve tangible morals out of mathematics.

My favorite story is the one about the universe, and how she came to be. I am a character in this story, and I am living my role. My thoughts, words, and actions have impact. When I die in this story, the particles that are me will scatter about the world and make more life, brighter stars, darker days, and new chapters.

I believe in faith. It is powerful, a subset of love — and it gives me strength when I most need it.

Strength is a complex thing.

People always talk about mothers who lift cars off of their babies. Science is what helps them accomplish the task. Love, and faith, is what makes them try in the first place.

I don't confuse the concepts of faith and knowledge, though I do use them as words of equal value because they are of equal import in my life. My faith doesn't spit at science, or laugh at math, or mock the wisdom of wise men no matter what label they took for themselves.

My faith is grounded in truth, but it is different than knowing.

I know the moon is about 3,470 kilometers in diameter, and I have faith that she fuels me with power.

I like to tell people about the moon, and how I have always loved her — back when I thought she could fit in the palm of my hand. Knowing the truth of her dimension makes her more real to me, but understanding that I am connected to her power means more than measurements.

I don't feel the need to weigh my faith, or prove it, or sell it.

I don't mind when someone tries to argue me out of it, but what argument stands against love? You can tell me that the people I love have made terrible choices. You could ask me complex hypothetical questions about rocks, and whether or not they can lift them. But it wouldn't change my love for them, or my faith in them.

You wouldn't expect it to, because love is a powerful force.

There are people out there who use the shields of love for their own personal gain and vendettas. Even someone like me, who believes in fairy tale reality, knows this to be true. These characters are written into the stories that built my framework of the world — how could they be forgotten?

An unkind queen sends her step-son to the depths of the forest under the guise of an unsurvivable hero's journey. His wife and her brother join him — bound by love. They fight monsters, complete their journey, and are guided home by the strength the moon has lent to her community of tiny families. There are no little characters in fairy tales. There are no small lights.

Good and bad are two constantly spinning dancers wrapped so tightly together that you hardly know where one starts and the other stops. It hardly matters which is which.

There is bad in me and there is good in me, and science could probably measure them — but the measurements would be mere footnotes of my faith. The only thing that matters is whether or not there is love in me.

Sometimes I lose sight of love — it buries away behind hurt and fear, but fellow believers bring it forth. It connects us the way leaves of a tree are connected to one another. We are rooted by old love. Fellow believers talk to me. They write. They assemble their thoughts, and they re-light my spark.

I use that spark to light a candle, and I place that candle on a pathway, outside in full view of my beloved moon.

It's a thank you to the universe for putting me in the presence of constantly refueled faith, and a thank you to the people who filled the world with particles of love. It is a beacon to everyone who needs to find their way home. It is a reminder to me that I am a piece of the universe, and that somewhere on the other side of the globe is a frightened girl lighting a candle to thank me for the things I did today that changed her world.

I am not a little character and it is not a little light.

It doesn't matter to me if someone else doesn't understand the reason I light that candle. It only matters that the person who needs the reminder sees it, even if that person is me.

It doesn't matter to me why I could lift a car off a loved one, it only matters that I would try.

My faith is like the moon.

It simply doesn't matter if you can quantify her power or understand why she shines.

It only matters that she does.

keep it up

If you're a mover, a shaker,
or a crafty craft-maker,
an artist, chance-taker,
or world forsaker...
If some call you freaky,
if you're super uniquey,
if you blog like a dino,
or invest in geekery...
If you're a doubter, believer,
comic book reader,
an avant-garde writer,
or an overachiever.
if you're a traveling actor,
or secret-thinktanker,
or a cryptozoologist,
or professional prankster...
Keep it up.

EGBO

Sometimes we stumble.
Sometimes we fall.
Worries nettle and panic resounds –

    if the wind blows just right,
    Life might stick like this forever.

Saturate yourself with hope till you are
too full for such worries. You will see :

Life keeps its own balance and not even
trouble stays in perpetual motion.

Energy transfers so lighten your load.
Let go of whatever prevents you from
charging yourself. Catch a burst, and
ride it through your journey of choice.

You will land.
You will stand.
You will see:

Life is on your side. The wind has
your back.

Everything's gonna be okay.

hand made

The bag I want is strong enough to hold the toddler who wants to ride in their auntie's magic purse. The bag I want hangs on my shoulders, trusting that shoulders like mine are ones you can rest easy on.

But the bags in the store are — absurdly — organized by color.

What color is best for holding books? A hundred adventurers, a thousand adventures?

I run a million scenarios through my mind. Shoes. Places. People. Nail color. Seasonal flora. Current trends. It is overwhelming so I try to think differently.

A blue box keeps the Doctor contained. A blue sky balances the clouds. Blue skin held Krishna in his humanity. Blue fur let Super Grover fly.

The bag I want is probably blue.

I seek the blue aisle and breathe it in for a moment, quieting my anxiety.

The bag I want is brave, infinitely more brave than I.

The bag I want will treat me gently. It will not pull my hair or press too firmly on my skin. It will not weigh me down, or hide my needs from me.

The purses in the blue aisle are organized by the mark of their maker. Some of those names are forged in fear: I avoid them. Fear can birth an illusion of strength, but I know it will not hold.

The salesperson pulls one down anyway. She runs her hands over the tiny decorative cut-outs lining the pockets. It is handmade, she says, and I know that to be true.

I've seen the small, punctured hands that bled to make it. How can I put all my resolutions--all my revolutions — in that bag when it is already so full of blood? How can I ask it to hold resistance at the ready, when it has only ever been taught how to hold its silence? How can I ask it to hold all my work when it has already borne more than its fair share of labor?

She shakes the bag toward me and it seems to groan. It is tired. I would be tired too, if I had seen the things it has seen.

"I would like a robot-made bag," I blurt, stepping away from her offering.

Ok, the salesperson soothes immediately, reading my body language, stepping away. She knocks a brown purse down accidentally. She tsks at it because it has found refuge in the safety of the blue aisle, but then, so have I.

I recognize the maker. I have seen the name on giant plastic cubes, full of clean water, shipped across long stretches of land. I have seen a little girl hug one of those boxes like it was a carnival teddy bear, rubbing her dry dirty face across the logo in snuggled joy, the dimples in the plastic leaving marks across her skin. She is going to name something important after the maker, she proclaimed then — her first born, or the first new-old plant she discovers.

That was years ago. She is studying to be a botanist now, and for all I know the maker hasn't made purses since all the way back when I first met the little scientist. When her hands were small, when my hands were still soft, when my shoulders were still untried.

It is an old bag. I can tell because it does not match the others. I can tell because the salesperson cringes as I reach out for it.

On the outside, it is ordinary but sturdy. On the inside, it is green and sparkly.

It rests easy on me, but can stand on its own. It is wide open, no busy and tiresome locks and zippers and buttons.

It is an old bag, but it is wide awake. It is ready.

"It is dinosaur-hearted," I tell the salesperson, and she nods in quick agreement, just to be free of me. We walk to the counter as I read the card tied to the purse, a card that discusses the importance of clean water.

The salesperson sees my interest and smiles. "A portion of the sales supposedly go to clean water efforts, but who really knows?"

I know.

And I think how differently the world would look if everything included a picture of the hands that made it, a picture of the hands it saved.

Surely then we wouldn't sort our purses by color?

you are loved.

We gather 'round from time to time, and share stories. Together, we are Tribe. Our perspectives and life-journeys weave around us like fireflies, and the dancing brightness illuminates every pathway — possible and impossible, alike.

I see the many ways we traveled to arrive here — and how easily it would be to arrive elsewhere — and I marvel at the synchronicity of our realities. Because, we are here now. We found each other.

My heart-fire is aflame, thanks to your
kindling, and in the brightness of its warmth
I see you as my connection to everything.

You ignite dreams.
You fuel kindness.
You are loved.

tangled universe

I believe in fixed points of time. The idea that some things are inevitable.

Yes. Free will is rampant, and — yes — daily choices are made at the micro-level in the span of a nanosecond, over and over again.

But, in the ever-evolving tapestry of life, some points are tied up by fate in advance, destined to make a knotted appearance no matter what the thread before it chooses to be or do.

A butterfly may decide to flap into a tornado, and all of China could jump up and down at the same time, and a little girl could blow dandelion fluff straight into a morning rain cloud, but none of these things would stop the world from sneezing— or make it quake— if the movement or stillness was intended to be a fixed point of time.

Moments, like choices, are sometimes unnoticed and often small, but never unimportant. Some of the most vital, ancient knots of destiny pass us by in a precious blink.

A breath of life. A step forward. A signature. A smile.

We can perceive the coming of these inevitable moments by paying attention to the appearance of extraordinary patterns in ordinary life. No matter how many threads appear — or how different they are — the closer to the core of kismet-kissed knot, the more they interrupt each other's stories. Tangles stand out. Maybe not at a cosmic level, but definitely from our solitary view — the perspective of one frayed part of one small string.

In those moments, I find comfort.

From my micro-view of Everything Ever, I can see that nothing I *did* threw life-as-we-know-it wildly off course.

Here, this, now—

is exactly where I am meant to be.

You have probably experienced the phenomenon, too. It works like this:

On Monday, you dream of yellow roses for no good reason. Maybe you've never even seen a yellow rose. On Tuesday, a stranger whistles "Yellow Rose of Texas" till you want to step on his toe to make it stop. Later that day, your car breaks down and you wait on a road you've never traveled— only to find yourself right beside a wild yellow rose bush. It makes you smile.

In that moment, you find intuitive understanding. This is your part in the knot.

The string of yellow roses was just temporarily twisted into your path, held tightly next to your journey. A glorious glitch in the Universe's great show.

And you had front row seats.

I've experienced these twists with alarming frequency lately and it's made me wonder how many glitches the dinosaurs witnessed before confronted with the fatal pop that faded them from emperors to memories.

Destiny is happily ambivalent to the casualties of its manifestations. But that's a worry best left to a more connected strand, or better yet — the Weaver–

the maker of looms–

the mother of the Fates herself.

The best I can do is string along and not be frayed down by the passing or fixing of time. And — when lucky enough to catch the Fates at work — bear witness to the journeys threaded through my own, take notice, and applaud.

Casualties aside, destiny deserves all the credit due any great artist.

Fate is a marvelous choreographer, and life is a frightfully wondrous — sometimes heartbreakingly shocking — show.

what if

What if the hurt of all those endings were actually labor pains
and a new universe is being born inside you?

What if all those fiery little hells turned out to be stars?

What if all that darkness was just a galaxy making space for itself?

What if that falling feeling is just a star inside of you
hoping to catch a wish?

What if one time
you wished for more wishes, and this is how it all plays out?

What if you are your own wish,
your own lucky star,

your own universe?

What then?

one second

Stop and listen — for one second.

You just experienced 9,192,671,770 periods of oscillation of an undisturbed cesium atom.

There's a real science-y explanation as to what that means, but I prefer the basically-science perspective.

Imagine the smallest thing your eyes can see and then think of something even smaller than the smallest fraction of it. So small, the eyes can't see it. So small, a microscope can't see it. So small, the Universe kept it a secret from humans for eons.

We found it, though, on one of our missions of boundless curiosity and we named it.

We call it a cesium atom.

When it thinks no one is looking, that atom dances — quick oscillations, swift movements. We watch quietly and keep tally of every twerk, boogie, and shimmy. On the 9 billionth, 192 millionth, 671 thousand, 7 hundred and 70th movement — we mark our time.

One second has passed.

In a manner of speaking, there is dancing in the air — and that dancing vibrates the universe as we are experiencing it. Vibrations make music and we set our clock by this microcosm of melody, capturing a symphony in every second.

And if you are still enough, you can hear it.

So stop and listen for just a second.

Isn't it beautiful?

best things

Sometimes you don't get a pony,
no matter how hard you pray.
And ice cream melts, and laughter dies,
and good moments fade away.

Sometimes you don't get a pony,
no matter which candles you blow,
and dreams are rocky, and rocks are heavy,
and there's no right way to go.

Sometimes you don't get a pony,
no matter what you do–
but sometimes not getting that pony
is the best thing to happen to you.

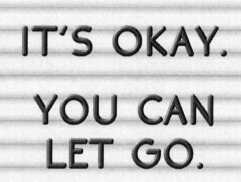

all beans

You'll have to let go of the cow to keep your palms wide open.

You'll need your palms wide open to accept the magic beans.

They will plant themselves in you, digging deep, cradling fascination and curiosity, between the grooves of your palms. Their enchantment is heavy. Their vision is quiet. Let their roots anchor you. Let them branch through your skin, and whisper to your heart.

You will grow wild, tangled, bewitchingly-magic beanstalks.

You will climb your way to adventures.

You will be charmed, you will be frightened. You will run, you will fall. But you will do all of these things on a path most are not lucky enough to ever even see.

And though you might never see the cow again, your adventure will lead you to the types of things you can hold with your palms wide open,

things born of the most enchanted parts of you.

freedom whistles

Anything can look gross from up close, but if you look even closer, most things become wondrous once again. It is an issue of science and the computations required to discover the perfect perspective. A detailed orchestration of diagonals and distance, measured to elevate the experience of beauty. At a certain angle, from a certain number of steps away, even your favorite source of beauty could look unappealing, or downright ugly, or worse — simply quiet. Can you imagine? To have something silenced when it could have spoken to you and shared its secrets with the very insides of your soul? Such is the power of distance.

For someone like me, life is as much about the observations as it is about the experiences. It's not that I don't have a little adventurer in my heart — it's that I have a giant scientist sitting on top of her. I am constantly calibrating my perspective — growing and shrinking the space between myself and my observations with a dexterity evolved from life-long practice. The decision to look closer or step farther is a crafted science I learned from my father, but the act of doing so is an art I picked up from my mama. I continue to study the science, and act the art into existence. The goal is not to change reality, hide from truth, or erase my acknowledgment of all the world's bad — but to shift a paradigm and to remember that everything under the sun has a place and purpose.

How it affects us on the outside is often unavoidable, but we can control how it speaks to our insides. We can translate it — changing what is whispered into a language that creates our best selves, and a landscape of our best possibility. Language is our legacy, after all — and, much like perspective, is a melody of science and art.

Today, the sun set over me.

Her rays warmed the air and her shimmering power stilled the clouds. Fragments of orange and silky webs of red-purple shot around in all directions, kissing the ground with pink light. The sun herself glorified in the show — radiating inward as much as outward — reveling in her great celestial roundness and yawning into her cosmic nap.

Below her, on the dusty plateau around me, a baby jackrabbit chased a pale green apple, paying no mind to the schedules of stars. He tried to capture the fruit, but its size was too great for his small eager hands and it would simply roll away. The little rabbit didn't seem to mind the chase — the treasured green prize was more than worth a weary hunt.

A hundred feet above his tall ears and grand adventures, a bird flew in circles, stretching her wings and enjoying this brief moment of time where her wingspan was larger than the sun.

She sang loudly, and her whistled song was about her freedom from everyone and her ownership of all the world. No one contested her tune or argued her claim, because no one could. Hers is a freedom that lives in her heart and an ownership of possibility that lives in her mind — and she is the only one who has power or providence there, in her insides, where the truth of her lives.

I mimicked her whistle and she approved — acknowledging my heart's freedom with a proud slant of her head. I nodded back and caught another glimpse of the little rabbit. He was focused on apples and even less interested in whistled freedoms than in the napping patterns of magnificent stars.

I let myself absorb the secrets of the Sleeper, the Hunter, and the Singer.

It required no shift of diagonal or distance because beauty such as theirs needs no elevation. Anyone who looks or listens will experience full measure of their truths — the sun's faith in the sanctity of cycles, the rabbit's dedication to the purity of the present moment, and the bird's reminder that every soul is as free as it believes itself to be.

So I continue forward in their honor, paying attention, search for beauty, and whistling the song of my freedom.

goals

Be just a little sillier

than you were the day before,

and tomorrow--

aim for twice as much,

plus a little more.

Try to cut your own hair.

Ask a stranger out.

Write a song or

rhymey poem

without a single doubt.

Plan a bit more silliness

than the world thinks it can stand,

and tomorrow,

no matter what, my dear,

remember what you planned.

endings fold

I've always been fascinated by Lasts.

The last piece of cake at a birthday party, the last worn book on the garage sale shelf, or even all the things I would do if I were one of the last humans on earth.

"The Last" is a tangible ending — not the sort that brushes by unnoticed. It does not whisper — it bangs, and it screams to the world, "Hear me now, see me now! I am the end, and I am the beginning." It is not the snake's mouth, or the tip of the tail. It is the *Last*, the space that holds the mouth and tail together, transforming a snake into an ouroboros, and a story into an eternity.

It is magical.

Today is the last day of the month and I am savoring it. The Earth will rotate completely around the sun before I see a shade or glimmer of this month again. It is a last, and I am mesmerized.

I feel this day stretching into a new page on the calendar, taking its time. It is yawning into its beginning, warming to the idea of a tomorrow where it does not exist as anything except a memory, and — even then — just a faded one.

Still, it toots its own horn, bangs its own drums, and sings its own swan song. It will be forgotten in due time, but time washes and fades everything, so it does not take the slight personally.

In fact, this day has nothing to say about tomorrow at all. It is simply celebrating how it was born of the grandeur of yesterday and rose to everything it could be.

In this month, people loved and told truths, saplings turned to trees, birds found some of the shiniest things, and balloons escaped into the heavens. And there were lies born, and knees scraped, and tragedies, and death. But most importantly — the world lived to the end of today's tale, and started to sparkle its way to the mouth of eternity.

A full circle begins again, and for this brief breath — we are forever.

Until tomorrow...

when we begin the spiral of madness, creation, and destruction again.

Tomorrow is a first,

the first day of a new month, and I will be celebrating.

I've always had a fascination with Firsts.

woven world

I've spent my day reading on the Internet, and the journey through words has pulled me through a rainbow of expressions and feels. I've been terrified, en-thralled, heart-warmed, and mystified. I've listened to songs, watched photo slideshows, broke the fourth wall with Deadpool, and saw a cat smack some-thing in the face. I've seen poets write prose, and stormtroopers write poems, and ducks draw cartoons. I've read words that sang, and heard silence that danced, and watched punctuation frost freshly baked ideas.

This part of the world, the invisible web that connects us, is my favorite treat. It is so very sweet.

When we play, when we write, when we share, I can almost see it — shimmer-ing like a child's laugh, glimmering like tears unshed, tangling sense into itself like ribbons on a May Pole.

The ribbons are beautiful as they pattern themselves, decorating even the smallest parts of my heart, allowing me to see even the most nano-nature of you.

You are a cloud of thought through their dance — magic down to the core of your most active molecules. You are energy — potential and kinetic. You are falling, floating, melting, imprinting, and flying through a sky that was made just for you.

You are a miracle, and I don't even want to blink. I don't want to miss a minute of your possibility.

So I won't.

Build a world with your words, and I will log in to read it because I am tangled into the pattern of our connection.

Somewhere at the center of us is an invisible web woven from magic. It is full of energy — soft in its motion, strong in its stillness — and, if you have faith, you can balance your way over the narrow threads.

I'll be walking them, too.

Closer to you, and the sparkling circuitry of your brilliance.

happiness stays

Happiness shined in front of my face, a dancing fluorescence. I drew her soft angles and bright center with my words, and as I scribbled, she giggled, whispering promises to never leave my side. In response, I promised I would write her story.

Her light warmed me and I leaned into her intangible presence. I rested my weary mind on her ephemeral softness and smiled to myself. It seemed as if strangers could see her glow glide softly against my skin, illuminating me the way the moon frames lovers on a lonely lake.

I wrote about her, and she posed for my writings — proud, large, beautiful, soft, and warm.

Then I blinked for just one second and the darkness behind my eyes — the darkness inside me — sang a lullaby that warmed me into a cozy sleep.

I was captured, and just one second became two minutes, and just two minutes became days. And I don't even know how long it was before I opened my eyes once more.

She was still there — a shimmering orb in the peripheral of my perception — and I was not surprised to find her waiting.

Even when caught in my own shadows, I could see her patient incandescence from the other side of my lids — reflecting the colors and shapes of hope on the black canvas of my darkness.

I worry that if I blink too slowly, I might lose her again.

So I focus.

Every day.

I ignore the haunting hums, calling me back to my dark. I open my eyes wide, pick up my pen and write her story — keeping the promise I made to her,

just as she kept the promise she made to me.

world pained

We call it world-pain — the chronic disease of the pure idealist, the invisible illness of the undiluted skeptic. It is a sickness of panic and rage, inflamed when the world isn't working as it ought.

When a child starves, when a species dies, when a lie spreads… the world aches, and the infected among us grieve with it, interwoven in companionship.

Don't hide from the pain.

At its center is an all-healing anti-virus, a quiet spark that burns helplessness like coal and brings light to a lost maxim of hope:

The world deserves better.

Let's give it our best.

let's go

You can carry this.

       You can do this.

You are strong enough for what they call magical, what they call dark,
      what they call imaginary, unjust, broken, dangerous, and dirty.

You've lifted Impossible above your head so often your muscles don't flinch
when you reach for more.

You've picked the crumble of unmovable mountains from your toes so often
that you sometimes don't even remember smashing through them.

You've lifted a few heavy sunrises too,
      high enough to light a day that fought so hard to be dark.

This just feels heavy because you've burned your hands, because you've lost
your shoes, because it might not be an Impossible of your choosing. This feels
heavy, but you can carry it, so let's go,

      let's go,

        let's go.

just broken

You're not tired, you're broken.

Your ankles are twisted and your body is bruised. The wind is in your face, pushing you down,

down,

so far down this mountain.

You're not tired. You're lost.

You thought you were going up, but you just jabbed yourself on the same rock for the second time. You're going in circles and the only thing you can do is hope that the circles are spiraling you up,

up,

to the top of this mountain.

You *think* you want to go up. You're not sure anymore.

You feel tired, but you're not. Truly.

You're not tired.

Your heart is crushed so flat it can barely beat. You're not tired.

Your lungs are sick of breathing in the contamination you ejected. You're not tired.

Your mind is hiding from the sheer magnitude of the world is it being forced to translate, but *you're not tired*.

You're just going somewhere, and the journey has been bumpy. There's been twisted paths and closed roads. There's been pitfalls and jagged edges.

Every injury caused by this journey has been healed by this journey. Every scar you had when you started, every wound you earned along the way, will be healed in the next few steps.

If you can make it.

You're slowing down. You're aching.   You can't see where you're going because there's blood in your eyes, sweat on your hands. You're slipping and everyone can see it...

But they can also see your destination, and how far you've come. Not a single person is worried that you'll fall. Not a single person is worried that you won't make it.

They see the calluses on your feet, and how those calluses did not weigh you down.

They see your eyes closing on your journey, but they know you're not lost, and you're certainly not tired.

You're just a little sweaty. You're just a little broken.

But none of that ever stopped you before.

You're just getting started, so keep going,

up,

up,

up.

You're going somewhere.

HARVEST
COMPASSION.

because i've had enough

Because I've had enough food, I am able to go hungry, for small bursts at a time. Because I've had enough Kindness, I am able to give it when I am completely out of reasons.

Because I've had enough, I know there is never enough. We are ever-refilling, ever-refillable.

Because I've had enough, I know there is always enough.

We are always full.

wild heart

My heart is the most wild thing about me. It goes where it wants, when it wants, to whom it wants, however it wants.

It is a fey creature, unpredictable and reckless. Brave, adrenaline-soaked, sweaty, manic,

happy.

My heart is the most wild thing about me, but it's caged inside me for safe keeping. My mind is a careful cage; my body, a safe one. There is padding for when my heart thrusts itself against my ribs in a burst of want. There are rolls and dimples for it to rest when it bruises and bleeds.

She is a wild heart, but a good one.

A kind one.

She loves people who do things, people who love things, people who hate things, people who aren't people at all.

She probably loves you.

Oh yes,

you.

If you get close enough to my heart for her to scent you, she will cuddle her gruesomely-callused body right alongside you. She will snuggle into your armpits and fall asleep listening to all your secrets, sniffing in the odors of your humanity.

She will keep your secrets, even when you eventually cut her open. And you *will* eventually cut her open.

Oh yes,

you.

It's almost impossible not to bruise such a brave and wild thing. She has been known to cut herself to hold more of you inside. She has been known to bruise herself trying to break through your cage and cuddle the core of you.

And she might bruise you, too.

Such a wild creature. Such a reckless one.

Such a hungry heart.

I cage her, for her own good. I protect her with cautious words, and careful thoughts, and lots of comfort food that line my ribs so that she will only hit padding when she tries to break through.

And she will try to break through.

She wants to get to know you better.

Oh yes,

you.

She probably loves you, after all.

HOLD ON
AS LONG AS
YOU WANT.

dreams sparkle

Life plays a perilous tune and the sad ballads can be as compelling as the sweet lullabies or the triumphant marches. Sometimes everyday ups and downs flip on themselves, and land on your dreams — crushing them into zillions of little pieces.

Sometimes, you have no choice but to walk through the shards of what used to be your hopes. The glimmering pieces were once part of something that made you whole — but now they just cut into your feet like glass, and slow you down.

You are built to survive, so you sweep them to the side. They were probably unlikely, you convince yourself — or perhaps impossible altogether. Over time, the pile is moved to the corner, and finally thrown away.

Then one day, you heal.

It might have been something you did, or it might have just been time — but you notice because suddenly, you can see it.

It sparkles.

A single shard. A single hope.

One solitary piece of a dream that was.

When you bring it to the light, it shines a rainbow of colors and pathways on the walls around you, expanding your world. It is a prism of paradigms and it calls to the sweetest lullabies of your heart.

The memory ripens until that solitary piece becomes part of a dream that is.

You hold on to the precious, misshapen memory of yesterday — and you step forward. Your scarred feet make you sure-footed in a way that you never were before. Life topples but you continue forward. As you walk, your ballad fades into your lullaby, and the lullaby strides into a call of victory.

You are triumphant, and your dream marches on.

good luck

It's hard to say when the day starts if you never sleep through a night. A day can start at 2pm. A day can start at 8pm.

Good morning. No matter what the sun is doing.

It's hard to say when a life starts once you've climbed out of the rubble of your past life, still breathing.

Good luck. Even if you did watch your dreams go up in flames.

Today I am feeling good. Like most words and emotional claims, I'm grading on a curve. Ten years ago, I might have called a day like this the worst day of my life. Today, I know better.

Some days are worse. Some days blink into such darkness that they can ignore the laws of the sun.

Good morning, if you're playing by those rules.

Good luck, if you're playing at all.

Good news: tomorrow is another day.

And you can start it whenever you want.

You don't have to wait for the little hand to finish its race, for the stars to go into hiding, or for the end of a sleep you could never seem to find. You can just call it good enough. You can just wish yourself good luck.

You can just tell yourself good morning. And a better day could be yours, just like that. Some days are inherently good.

Some days wink into such brilliance that the sun itself becomes a shadow.

Good luck, my friend.

May your life blink through enough days that you can see all the dreams of your past life still hanging on the stars.

Good morning, my friend.

May your day be so full of light you do not need the sun to tell you when your life begins.

It begins now.

look up

The answer is seemingly lost in the abyss but we sense it —
sparkling and peeking through the darkness,
playing a galactic game

of hide-n-seek.

No answer stays hidden forever.

No one plays the game of life alone.

Together, we seek and find.

the knowing

My teardrops don't fall like rain. They blow away, swimming through the wind like wishes made on dandelion fluff. They float away, following their own pathway, pretending they came from their own unique spark in the universe.

Mine choose to land on your words.

They pour down my cheeks, splashing paper, smearing graphite. I was laughing ten minutes ago but my throat is buttoned shut now.

You were supposed to be okay, but I know.

I know you're not.   I know it's not.

And *it's okay to not be okay*. I know that, too.

I know things. *I've seen things.*

I don't know what you're going through, though. I've held troubles, but they weren't shaped like yours. I've lost, but none of my missing pieces would have filled your gaps.

I know some things, not all things.

I know I want to be here for you. I want to ease what I can. I want to give you the words I don't have, and the hugs I know you can't even feel right now. I want, I want, I want...

Nothing *I want* matters right now, and it's important for you to know that.

It's important for you to know that it's okay to not be okay. It's important for you to remember that you know things.

You've seen things.

You will survive this. All the things that aren't okay will one day be okay again, and that'll be okay, too.

I'll be here either way, and you can rest with me. You can tell me your stories, even the worst ones.

You can't scare me. I've seen things. I know things.

I survive things.

And even though it may not feel like it right now...

So do you.

bleeding gratitude

My heart is crying.

I am thankful to be so connected to others that I am able to suffer the scratchy pain of separation. I am blessed to have friends and family to miss so badly.

I am bruised.

I am grateful for the forgiving nature of my life-source — how it finds a way to speak silently of the wounds I've collected, and how it heals me anyway.

I am skin-burnt and ever-so-thankful for the sun, and the gift of small freedom which allows me to see her.

I am thankful for the infinity of freedom, no matter how small the drop.

I hear the current of our connection. I am grateful for the skill of listening.

I am changed— an entirely different person today than I was yesterday. I am thankful for my confidence that the world will still hold me kindly.

I am grateful for the possibility of unconditional love, and the hearts who give it to me in abundance, and the knowledge that all such love is rooted in the same powerful earth.

I am grateful for the benefit of vision. I see love everywhere.

I am grateful for your love — it shines like the sun, forgives like my life source, and heals all things with time. My heart aches today and it is changed but still — still — it beats with gratitude for you.

Unconditionally.

untold stories

I want to write about something happy, but a funny thing happens when I'm writing.

I start to tell myself the truth.

As soon as I start typing, I know that I will be led astray. Somehow my words always take me to the truth that wants telling, rather than the stories I want to share.

But untold stories don't want to live inside me. I am a bad host, an infertile garden. Stories don't blossom in my heart, they need to be spoken into my world.

My heart is heavy lately. It is not a garden, it is a jar and I fill it with things. I fill it constantly.

I don't want to write because it makes a funny thing happen.

I start to remove the lies.

The careful little ones that decorate my atmosphere. The ones I tell myself I believe. Everything is going to be okay, my jar is labeled. But if I write enough words, that label might fall off.

There are few beliefs of my own that I can count on. Common ones, like how I know that I will defend my friends to the very end. Uncommon ones, like my love of balloons.

Sometimes I think about helium balloons, and how they're going extinct. It's a complex thing, relating to economic systems and caps, byproducts of products regulated by places outside of our control. It has to do with the availability of a resource that will need to be so expensive that it creates its own extinction.

It made me think of rarity.

Rara avis is Latin, for rare bird. I've shortened it to Ra Avis and I use it everywhere as my name, though my real one is inky and distinct — centuries old, and centuries young. It will exist long after I am gone.

Names are not so fleeting as the things I have loved.

I've loved balloons my whole life. The giant kind. The tiny ones. The ones that are filled with confetti and the ones dipped in gold. I like the kind that are plain and simple, and the ones that you can get from grocery stores and realtors just by asking. I love balloons, yet I never have any problem letting them go. I just open my hand and trust that it's the right thing to do, for me.

Balloons are beautiful.

They're lighter than air, the way the worries should be.

They're shaped by their insides, the way we are.

Balloons are fleeting, by their very nature, but circumstances of the world around them are making them extinct.

Our grandchildren's grandchildren may never know what it is to hold one that can fly. They may never know what it is to fill one. They may never know what it is to let one go.

They may never know that sometimes you don't let balloons go, sometimes they just slip away, and the only thing left for you to do is be okay with it.

Yes, sometimes balloons let *you* go.

Be okay with it.

The balloon tied to your birthday table wasn't your birthday. It wasn't your year or your life. It was just a moment, and moments are fleeting.

The balloon tied to your car wasn't your wedding. It wasn't your marriage or your happily ever after. It was just a symbol, and symbols live even when they are gone.

The balloon you loved so preciously loved you too, but it had to go. It was headed somewhere, even if you don't know where.

You're headed somewhere, too.

Even if you don't know where.

Don't worry. Love goes with you.

Everything is going somewhere. The world is in constant motion. One day, in the future, balloons will no longer be lighter than air. They'll be filled, like us, with hot air and love and heavy moments. Tomorrow will be very different, and yesterday will just be one more fleeting thing we've had to let go.

Yesterday is on its way to today. Today is headed toward whatever it is going to be.

It's going to be okay.

Everything's going to be okay.

Well, look at that.

I was so afraid to write, afraid of where I was going, but it turns out my heart knew all along. Hearts are such funny things. They get heavier and heavier from the love they store, and somehow that makes them lighter.

Lighter than air. The way worries should be.   The way worries are —

 if you are just brave enough to let them go.

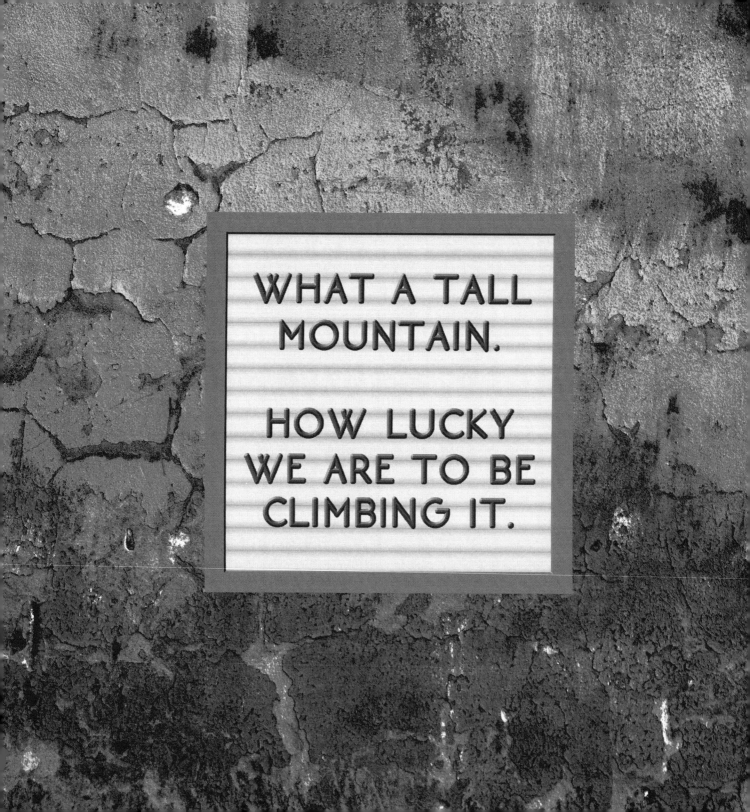

teardrop confetti

I used to carry confetti in my pocket,
ready for a reason to celebrate anything.
Then the storm came
and the little pieces of tissue melted away.

I tried to catch the flood-
grab the raindrops that fell sweetest...
because God was crying
and the tears were holy
and my hands are sanctum
made,
like all hands,
for holding faith.

I saved the drops in my pocket,
and they turned to blessings,

Little pieces of poetry.

I collect their reflections,
the sanctity of their spilling:

I am ready to celebrate
everything.

family time

My family would keep calendars on the wall for months. There was always a reason. Dad liked the flowers on top of the April calendar. Mama wrote an important number on January 10th. My little sister ate July and then we would forget about August by the time we came to it.

I have an odd relationship to time.   My year flipped over while I wasn't looking, but perhaps that's because my time is not quite my own. I live with Mama now, on her Unstandard Time.

Today she made an appointment for us at 5:15pm. I work till 5:15pm, so in essence — Mama made an appointment for us to be late. There was traffic because there's always traffic in Southern California on a weekday just after work and a two minute drive became a twenty minute drive. Sometimes, I leave work early. Every so often, a street is unblocked.

Theoretically, she claimed, we could get there on time.

Time is a gamble to her.

And my mama rolls hard.

I imagine, in her mind, time is a casino. Every minute is a wild games of chance, or a precious illusion of skill. She's feeling lucky today — every day — with chips falling from her pockets like rainfall. She has a chip for every day she survived, and she winks at the dealer before going all in.

Is she bluffing?

I've known her my whole life and your guess is as good as mine. She has a poker face when she plays her days, no matter the cards she is dealt.

I know how this game ends, in the end. I know the house always wins, but I stopped trying to argue my point years ago, long before my little sister stopped eating the calendar pages.

At least... I'm pretty sure she stopped eating the calendar pages.

Now that I think of it, I've never seen one hanging in her house either, and it wouldn't surprise me if she snacked it away, or burned pieces of it in rebellion of time itself.

Everyone in my family has an odd relationship to time.

home rooted

Home is imperfections running wildly — stomping muddy footprints across the flooring of your heart.

Home is loud traditions celebrated too early or too late, with just the right amount of love.

Home is where you are recognized for your molten core and your dazzling shine, in equal measure.

Home is the Knowing. The sun will pierce through darkness, the moon will smile with the stars, and you will survive the coldest depths of today's winter because the warmth of yesterday and shine of tomorrow seeps through it all.

Home is the ground beneath you, wherever you are,

and the light that dances forward, guiding you wherever you go.

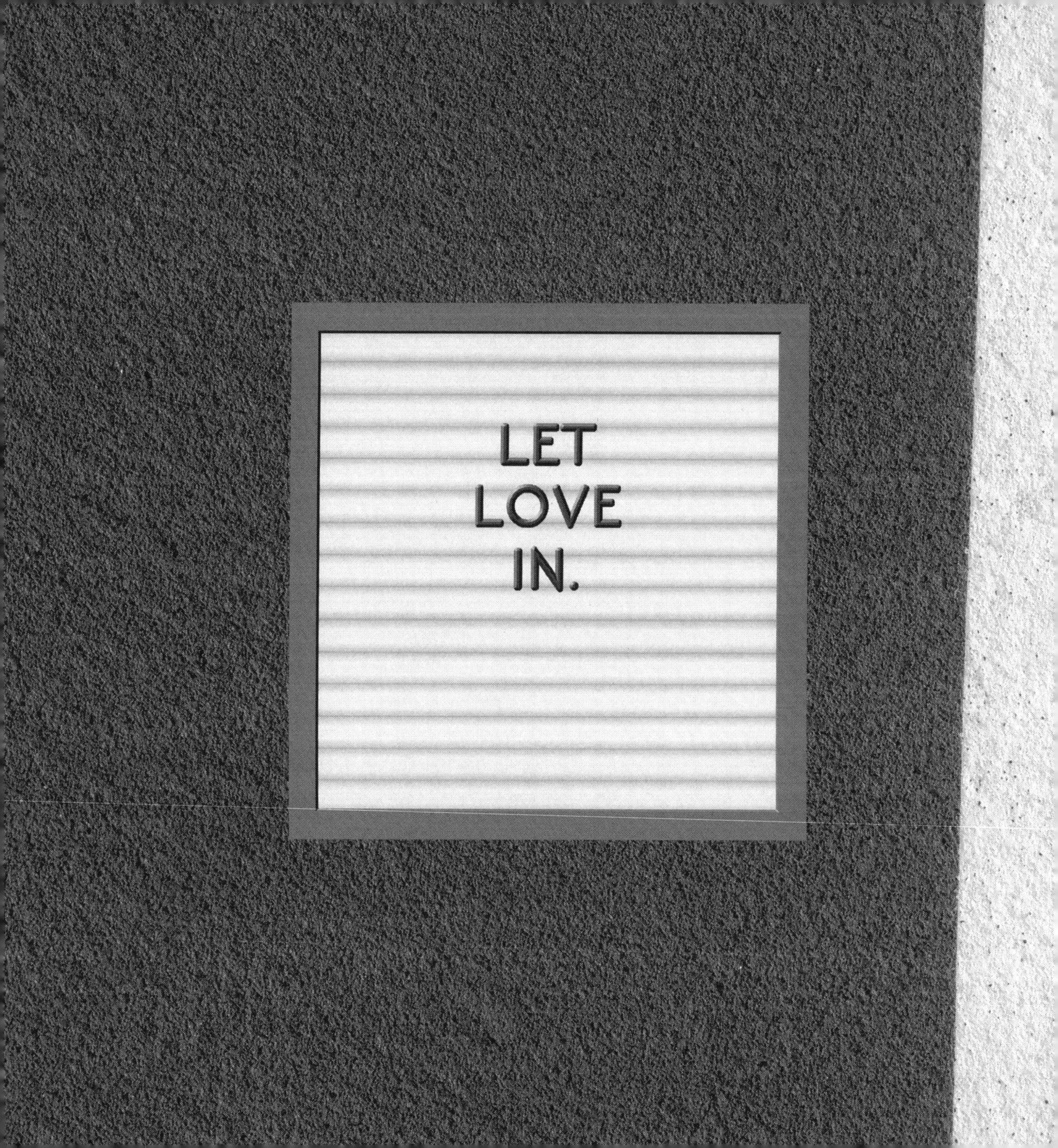
LET
LOVE
IN.

poetry passing

"Do you read a lot of poetry?" he says, nodding toward my stack of books, making idle conversation as he refills my lemonade and sets out my napkin and utensils. He's struck the balance just right — personal but not intimate, professional but not recited. His comments are focused on the books on the table, not my tear-stained cheeks or the dinosaurs falling out of my purse. I know how he will respond, how he will flex to my response, because there is a pattern to him.

He is poetry.

Everyone is.

I read a lot of poetry. Neruda, Cummings, Eliot, Wilcox, Silverstein, Whitman... you.

In the mornings, I drive to work with mama. She is a haiku and I feel almost sorry for the people who don't understand how the structure of her is designed to be self-sustaining, to fold up upon itself. They re-read her lines as if her story can be found in the confines of the structure, as if the simplicity wasn't just a guise for a complex juxtaposition.

Lines, unseen.
Heart, beats uncounted.
She, a poem.

I read a lot of poetry. I was born from it.

In the mornings, I drive 28 miles to work, I pass a thousand cars, and it is like flipping through an anthology of poems. Sometimes a stanza catches me and I stare through my window, through their window, into their eyes. I read their poem backwards, then forwards again. Their poetry moves in ways cars do not allow, in ways the California Highway Patrol does not allow. The words ebb against me and the lines flow with me.

Life is moving water,
and poetry is motion,
We all swim our stanzas,
but some see the ocean.

People are poetry.   Everyone.

I read a lot of poems.

In the mornings, I reply to my emails, sending messages to my friends. This one is a limerick, this one an epic poem. This one might be a classic one day, a poem that all other poems carry in their heart. This one rhymes with me. It's not a perfect rhyme, but we are jagged, broken in the same way. In the cosmic table of contents, we are filed under the same words, and it is no wonder that our feet found their way to the same streets. The universe is an organized thing despite all the seeming randomness.

It is no easy job to hold so much poetry, and that is why her stars die and explode into flame. That is why she orbits, why she spins. That is why she has cavernous holes within herself that eat away everything she thought she knew, and that is why she knows so little that she continues to expand.

There is so much poetry in this universe, *in you.*

> *You are life:*
> *an exploding star,*
> *a black hole,*
> *a swimming*
> *floating,*
> *poem.*

If I have not read you yet, I will, even if it is only as you pass me by.

I read a lot of poetry.

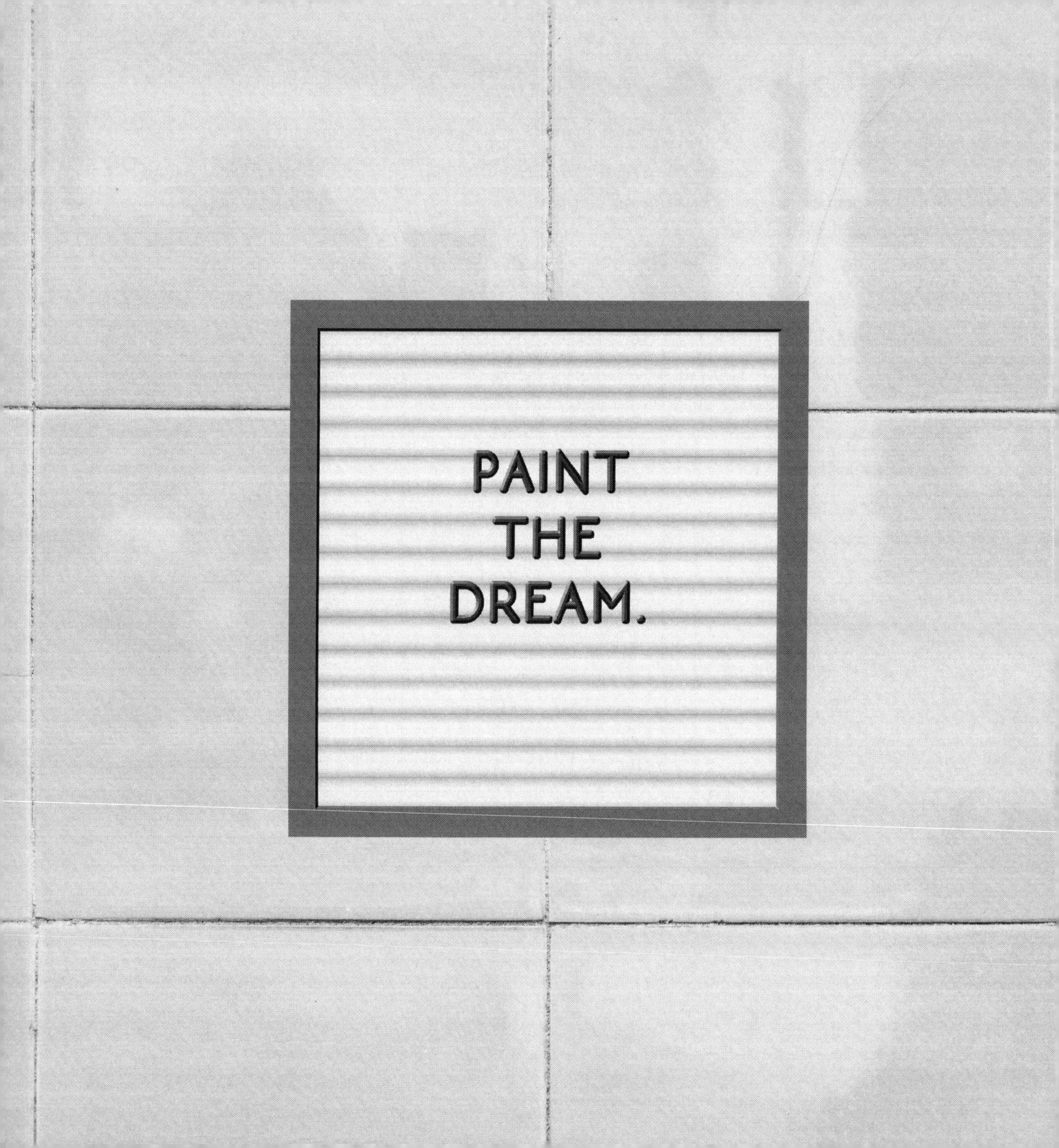
PAINT
THE
DREAM.

mulberry street

There's probably a mermaid out there in the water.

There might be a daisy on the sun.

Yesterday, I curled up under a Christmas tree and saw magic blink by. It could have been a faerie.

It may have been a gnome.

Today, an Elvis song started at the exact same moment as the rain.

It seemed to be raining water, but there may have been diamonds in there, too. It might have been apple juice. The rain itself might be the sweat of a dragon flying close to the sun, hoping to make a wish on a star-weed.

It might be the splashes of a cryptid, visiting a cousin cloud.

Don't look straight at magic.

You'll never see it clearly that way.

There's so much that happens just out of sight and to see it right, you'll have to close your eyes
and look with your heart.

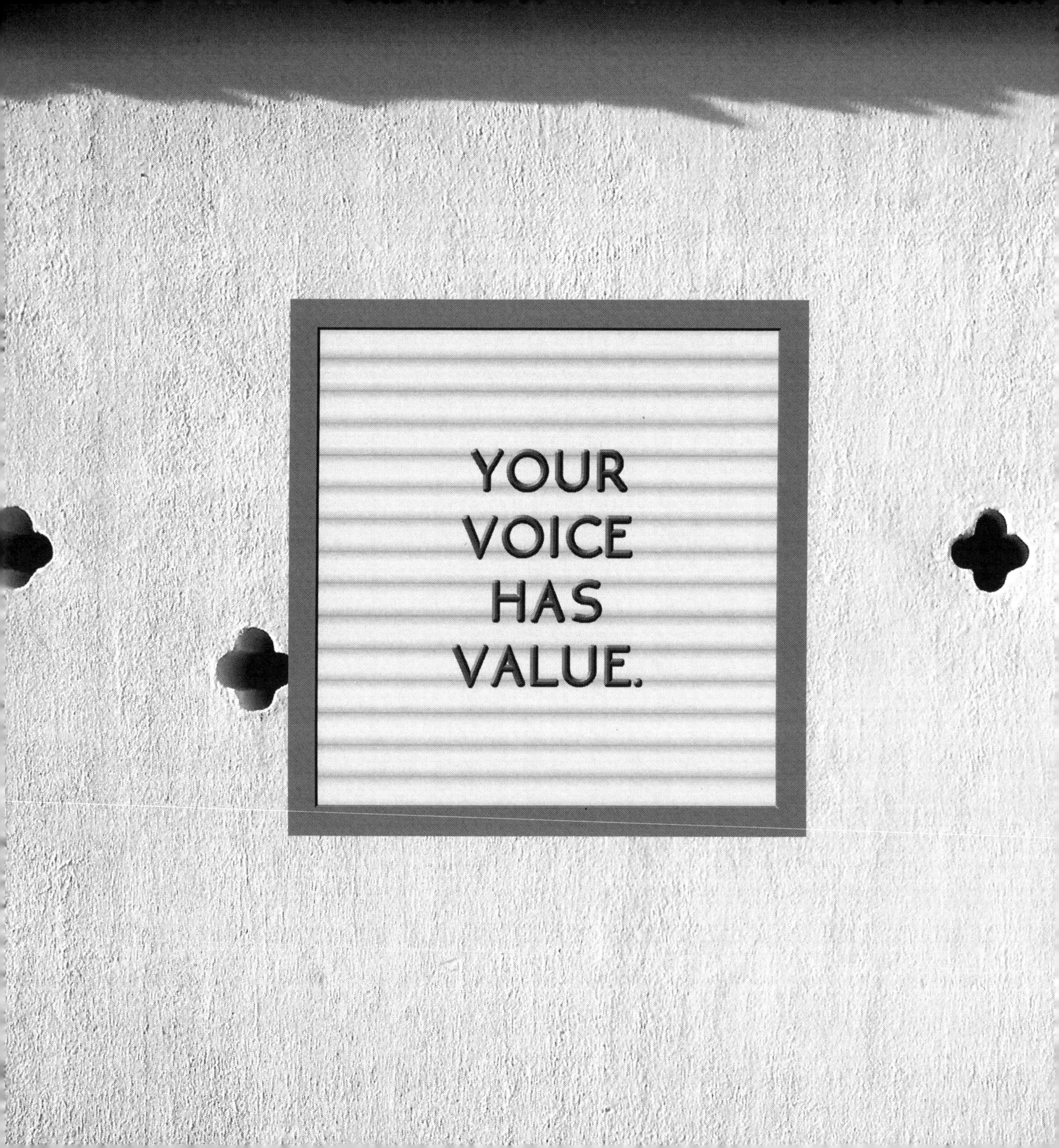
YOUR
VOICE
HAS
VALUE.

new year

The sun goes down in one year and rises in the next. Happy New Year, no matter what day it is.

Every new year welcomes a beginning, and beginnings are precious to me.

I've made too many mistakes and survived too many tragedies, to scoff in the face of any fresh start, regardless of its place on a calendar.

In the turning of an old year to a new one, the universe is at the apex of every possible future, and anything we want left behind is locked away behind the doors of yesteryear. The world calls out to us — let go of regrets and step forward.

It is a transition worthy of celebration. Greatness and wonder are just ahead of us, waiting patiently for us to reach them.

Our mistakes were just short pathways to these bigger, more glorious journeys.

The first step of which starts now. At the beginning.

So give thanks to the tragedy that has given your year substance, and say goodbye to it. Find peace. Then roll memories up into a firecracker, and set them aflame with your hopes. As they burn to ash, your dreams will fill the sky with fiery patterns of color and light.

The sound of the sky popping is your mighty roar to cosmos — letting Fate know to be ready for you, because you are blazing toward her.

And when tomorrow dawns, don't forget to smile at the sky, in gratitude for the gift of yet another wonderful beginning.

early girl

The time is now, and it is yours.
Wake up and drink in dreams.
The world is full of joy for you,
bursting from the seams.

We've been saving all the Stories for you
and all your future friends,
so you'll be strong when the world cracks,
because you'll know how well it mends.

Fill yourself on love and magic —
burp up a world-wide hug.
Be brave, lucky one, we've waited for you:
so chug,
chug,
chug.

PUT FEET
ON HOPE.

frightfully wondrous

I wish I wrote the way I read: unforgivingly, relentlessly, visibly. I trace my fingers over letters, mouth the words, gasp and cry. I slam books shut in a way that only other readers understand. A slow, two-handed slam where the letters press together hard enough to send a poof of scented air toward my face. It smells like the story, aged and fantastical, and I always open the book again. I'm stained, you see, and stains return to stain.

I've told a thousand stories to myself the last ten days, some to soothe, some to repeatedly and achingly wake me from peaceful slumber. Those stories don't stain my conscious mind, just my dreaming one. I am forgiving and clumsy in the way I tell tale. I am invisible in the way I write. The ink is scrawled on the inner linings of my heart and you can only read it when life gives me lemons. The juice spills over me and suddenly I can read my story and — oh — how I read.

I read voraciously, unforgivingly, relentlessly, visibly, and my story stains me twice. I slam the book and it wakes me from my nightmares,

scenting my day with lemon and a copper that could be blood.

There's a lifetime in that burst, and every story is all mixed together. A younger version of me picked a basket of lemons from below a tree, and washed them in well water. My hands gently pressed over the rind, rubbing the dirt from the pores. I had perfect balance in this effort. They didn't slip or bruise. I have good hands for some things. Later, I would ask my big sister to sort them, and my little brother to free them of leaves. Later I would watch my big brother slice them with cool efficiency, and watch my baby brother and baby sister squeeze them into a bowl for him with more enthusiasm than a human body should be able to hold. My hands weren't right for the other parts of the process. My hands aren't artistic, aggressive, or discerning, but they washed that lemon well, and they loved that lemon as it was.

In that moment, I felt as if everything was right with the world. It seemed as if the right things for me might just simply fall from trees, land at my feet, and guide my path. My hands felt capable — fearfully and wonderfully made.

I laughed into that well, the happiness of it shaking like pennies into its pit, and maybe it was a wishing well, and maybe my laugh sounded like a heart-born plea for more because I've certainly had my share of lemons.

I'd like to think I still hold them well. I'd like to think they are given to me because my hands were made to hold them.

It is a story I tell myself, just another I write with invisible ink, just another dream I read with forgiveness.

I wish I could write that tale more boldly. I wish I could make pages of words you could slam together, the way readers like me do. It would poof toward you then, and you'd scent my quietest tales. The ones that smell like copper, like wishing-well pennies, like blood. The ones that smell like a lifetime of lemons, and the miracle of a thousand perfectly-made hands.

But then you'd be a little stained, and the lemon juice might make visible your secret stories, and your hands might never stop smelling like a penny that might one day be a wish.

On a hard enough day, lost in a big enough story, everything smells like wishes eventually — all of it — the dreams, the memories, and even — mysteriously — this book.

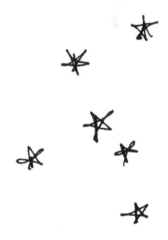

a note from rara

Best Beloved,

The words in this book have been cherry-picked from over five years of blogs, social media posts, and messages of love. It is my hope that they will inspire tangled conversations, acts of healing, and words of compassion. Thank you for reading. Thank you for existing.

I have so much hope for your tomorrow. I know you are building a beautiful world and the most beautiful version of yourself. May your efforts be gentle with you. May your journey be rewarding. We are all rooting for you.

My complete contact information can be found at Rarasaur.com. If you reach out, I promise, I will reach back.

Ra Avis ♡

They'll say you gotta iron your shirt
and keep your hair so long.
And they'll say you gotta wear a bra,
then they'll say you're doing it ~~wor~~ wrong.
And they'll say your body don't need touch,
that your belly don't need cake.
They'll say you can't and shouldn't...
and that is their mistake.

Oh! to be like Time —
and never make a
milestone out of a molehill.
and never make
a mountain
out of a minute.
Oh to be like Time —
and effortlessly march forward.

You be
you.
You is
awesome.

Oh! to be as the sky!
and wear purple
when
every-
body-
every-
where
expects
black.

You ARE Loved!

You don't need
to draw fences
around your smiles.
You don't need to
put spaces between
your seeds. The
burning core of earth is
no limit. You have bloomed
through fires, you have
danced through dark. This
might be a good place to dig
for roots so don't be afraid.
Reach out. Grow free. Grow deep.

My universe is made of tiny stories.
They blossom like dandelions in the
cracks of a life I paved with my
own hands. The roots hurt, but they
are strong. They are weeds but they
blossom bright. They die, eventually,
but they leave behind the possibility
of wishes.

"This too?!"
We cry, in grief.
"This too!!"
We chant belief.
The clouds reply,
caress erasing sky,
Whispering
    "Everything,
      everything,
      this too."

Not even
the sky
gets to stay
the same.

I am not a poet
    but the universe
has written me into a poem or two.

I am not a poet
    but I've kissed the sun
So I am a poem...

Like you.

The ocean sparkles like treasure below,
the stars are like diamonds above.
And you, my friend, are precious too.
You are loved. You are Loved.
You are love.

Clouds never forget
they are clouds, not even
when they float away
or when their loves fade
into the sky. Clouds never forget
the shape they were when
they knew you, the shape you saw
in them, and the shapes they could be.
Clouds never forget ...
and maybe that's why they cry so much.

Healing has no last page, no finish line.

We're constantly being asked to pull the cure for a broken world out of our hearts, but there's no magic word.

If there were, it would have been uttered by now— sobbed by a child covered in shrapnel, prayed by a woman watching her village burn, typed into a legal document by someone not able-bodied enough to shout it on a witness stand.

There is no quick-sip antidote. Peace is just something we work toward, every day. It's about the things we can become. It's about the things we should un-become. It's about changing our hearts when they need change, no matter how scary that is.

The secrets to mending broken people are not delivered by missiles, or shouted from podiums— they are whispered to children, pressed into today by yesterday's fingerprints. The secrets to healing are lullabies that the universe provides, so I sing them, I sing them, I sing them.

All day long, forever. You are loved.

You are loved. You are loved.

THE
UNIVERSE
PROVIDES.

Made in the USA
San Bernardino, CA
15 June 2018